THE CANADIAN

This edition published by
W H Smith Publishers, Canada

Produced by
Bison Books Ltd.
Kimbolton House
117 A Fulham Rd.
London SW3 6RL

Copyright © 1989 Bison Books Ltd.

ISBN 0-88665-562-5

Printed in Hong Kong

ROCKIES

TEXT	JEAN CHIARAMONTE MARTIN
DESIGN	MIKE ROSE

B. Mitchell

To Holly

*3/6 Mount Assiniboine and Lake Magog, Mount As-
siniboine Provincial Park, British Columbia.*

INTRODUCTION

The Canadian Rockies extend for about 800 km (500 mi) from Waterton Lakes National Park on the US border to the inaccessible wilderness north of Jasper National Park. They follow the Continental Divide, which also describes the border between British Columbia and Alberta, and average only 80 km (50 mi) wide, bordered on the east by the plains and on the west by a deep valley called the Rocky Mountain Trench. All mountain ranges to the east of the trench are part of the Rockies, but the ranges to the west are part of the Columbias, much older mountains which include the Selkirks, Purcells, Cariboos, and Monashees.

The greatest prizes of the Canadian National Park System are here: Banff, Jasper, and Waterton Lakes on the east slope of the Rockies in Alberta; Kootenay and Yoho on the west slope, in British Columbia; and Glacier and Mount Revelstoke in the Selkirks. Numerous provincial parks dot the area, including Mount Robson, Mount Assiniboine, Lougheed, and Bugaboo. Wilderness areas, completely undeveloped for tourism, include Ghost River, Siffleur, White Goat, and Willmore Wilderness in Alberta, and the Purcell Wilderness Conservancy in British Columbia. Tourists travelling throughout the mountains can find everything from nineteenth-century resorts with golf courses and ski slopes to vast areas containing no improvements but narrow footpaths.

The Canadian Rockies were the result of a period of uplift which began about 70 million years ago, caused by the tremendous forces created by drifting continents. As the North American continental plate moved slowly westward, away from the Eurasian plate, it began to press against the eastward-moving Pacific plate. The great pressures created by this movement found an outlet in a fault line, later to become the Rocky Mountain Trench, and the flat land to the east of it buckled, broke and was forced upwards into sharp peaks. The Columbias are some three times older than the Rockies, and all those extra eons of erosion exposed layers of metamorphic rock which still lay below the sedimentary surface of the relatively young Rockies.

Wind, water, and frost immediately began to shape the new mountains, and the glaciers of the Ice Age carved out a characteristic landscape of moraines, cirques, and arêtes. Great icefields and glaciers still cover vast areas of the Canadian Rockies, scouring mountain valleys, filling streams and lakes with their melt, and depositing rubble as they imperceptibly advance and retreat through the ages.

The first European to cross the Rockies was David Thompson, of the North West Company in Montreal. The fur trading company had established a trading post at the foot of the Rockies in 1799, and in 1806 Thompson was despatched to explore the Columbia River, to ascertain whether it could be used to transport furs to the coast. Finally, in the winter of 1810, Thompson crossed the Rockies by way of Athabasca Pass, in what is now Jasper National Park, and by 1811 reached the mouth of the river, on the Pacific Ocean, thus opening up a new trade route.

Competition between the Americans and the British (of the Hudson's Bay Company) for control of the Rocky Mountain fur trade was fierce in the early nineteenth century. This was the era of the mountain men, a handful of daring men who made a living roaming the high wilderness, trapping beaver to sell skins to the trading companies or to trade for goods. By 1845 beaver had become scarce and demand had died down, and this era gave way to the gold rush years.

In the 1850s and 1860s the Fraser River and the Cariboo valleys were the sites of a frenzied gold rush, where some claims amounted to over a million dollars. Thousands of hopeful prospectors flooded tiny frontier towns, hoping to strike it rich. The North-West Mounted Police, forerunner of the 'Mounties', was formed in 1875 to keep law and order on the frontier. They managed to control the whiskey trade and made treaties with local Indian tribes. Consequently the Canadian West was much more peaceful than the Wild West of the United States.

Eventually the placer mines were played out, and a new era of settlement began with the completion of the Canadian Pacific Railway in 1885. The last spike was hammered at Craigellachie in the Selkirks of British Columbia on 7 November 1885, connecting the East and West coasts and opening the interior to ranchers, farmers, miners, loggers, and other pioneers. Immigrants from the East Coast and from Europe, from the West Coast and from Japan and China arrived in large numbers, changing the face of the country with homesteads, farms, and mines.

To protect the precious wilderness of the high country, and to market the beauty of the area to wealthy tourists, in 1885 the Canadian government established a 26-sq km (10-sq mi) park around the Cave and Basin Hot Springs, in what is now Banff National Park, to be developed as a European-style spa. In 1887 the area was expanded to 670 sq km (260 sq mi) and officially became Canada's first national park. In 1930 it was enlarged again to its present size, 6640 sq km (2564 sq mi). Other national parks followed soon after, including what were to grow and become Yoho (1886), Glacier (1886), Waterton Lakes (1895), Jasper (1907), Mount Revelstoke (1914), and Kootenay (1920). The establishment of numerous provincial parks in the years to come would ensure that the grandeur and pristine beauty of the mountains would be preserved for all to enjoy.

The park systems have also guaranteed that the native flora and fauna can flourish, unhindered by the encroachment of man. Wildflowers abound in a riot of colours in the valleys and uplands during the summer months. Such large mammals as black and grizzly bear, elk, deer, moose, Rocky Mountain goat and bighorn sheep frequent the parks, as do cougar and bobcat and many small mammals such as porcupine, beaver, Columbian ground squirrel, hoary marmot and snowshoe hare. Over 220 kinds of birds inhabit the parks, from the majestic golden eagle to the diminutive mountain bluebird. A patient and quiet visitor can observe a variety of wildlife, especially if he is willing to wander away from the car parks and observation points into the wilderness. Out there, where the only sound is the wind, the rustle of leaves, or the gentle rush of a stream, lies the real magic of the Rockies.

BANFF

Banff National Park in Alberta presents some of the world's most exquisite alpine scenery. The jewel of Canada's park system, it attracts visitors from all over the world, and is a source of pride to Canadians from every province. Three ski resorts (Norquay, Sunshine, and Lake Louise), some 1300 km (780 mi) of hiking trails, numerous bridle paths, and canoe and bicycle rentals ensure that novice as well as experienced outdoorsmen can actively enjoy the beauty of the mountains.

Sir George Simpson of the Hudson's Bay Company was the first explorer to cross the Banff high country, in 1841. The first thorough exploration of the area was carried out in 1858-59 by geologist James Hector, who discovered Kicking Horse Pass, the route by which the Canadian Pacific Railway (and later the Trans-Canada Highway) would traverse the mountains.

With the arrival of the railway in 1885 came the establishment by the government of the Hot Springs Reserve, centred on the Cave and Basin Hot Springs (recently restored and reopened). A resort area soon grew to accommodate wealthy visitors carried westward by the new railroad. It was named after Banffshire, the Scottish birthplace of Lord Strathcona, the railroad's president. European-style spa resorts, the Banff Springs Hotel and Chateau Lake Louise, were built for these fashionable tourists, and today tourists can still enjoy these hotels in their luxurious settings beneath the mountains.

The reserve was greatly expanded in 1887 and renamed Rocky Mountain National Park, and in 1892 the Lake Louise area was added, named for the daughter of Queen Victoria (for whom the glacier at the end of the lake was named). In 1930 the park reached its present size and was given its current name. By then roads were being built that would open the parks of the West to all Canadians. Today Banff is so popular that the best way to experience the natural tranquillity of the mountains is to take a walk to one of the charming teahouses reminiscent of the railway era, or a lengthy hike in the backcountry.

Banff is a sightseer's paradise, from the delightful setting of Banff townsite, ringed by five mountains (Rundle, Tunnel, Cascade, Norquay, and Sulphur) to the famous view across Lake Louise to Victoria Glacier. Moraine Lake, in the superb Valley of Ten Peaks, is a popular destination, as is the Vermilion Lakes area, where wildlife can often be seen.

Lined by dramatic peaks, the Bow Valley Parkway becomes the Icefields Parkway at Lake Louise. At Bow Summit, 40 km (24 mi) north of Lake Louise, the road enters the beautiful Mistaya Valley. A short walk from Bow Summit ends at a breathtaking viewpoint over Peyto Lake, coloured dazzling blue by glacial melt as are so many alpine lakes in the Rockies. Continuing north along the Saskatchewan River, surrounded by glacier-laden crests, the road passes Mount Athabasca on the Continental Divide and leaves Banff, the heart of the Canadian Rockies.

15 The peerless view across emerald-green Lake Louise to Victoria Glacier.

16/17 The Bow River meanders through the broad green Bow Valley, as seen from the Banff Springs Hotel.

18/19 Banff townsite occupies a stunning position, bordered by an evergreen forest and the Bow River on one side and the heights of Mount Rundle and Cascade Mountain on the other.

20 Mountain avens carpet the shoreline of Glacier Lake below Southeast Lyell Glacier.

21 top A stand of brilliant yellow aspens colours the valley below Mount Rundle in autumn.

21 bottom Alpine larch is common at high elevations in the park. In autumn the needles turn bright yellow before falling off. These larches are near Eiffel Lake.

22/23 The Banff Springs Hotel in its spectacular wooded setting. The white water on the right is Bow Falls.

24/25 Red and white canoes at rest on Lake Louise, with Mount Victoria in the background.

26/27 Canoers drift down the Bow River below the towering mass of Castle Mountain.

28 Young bighorn sheep skillfully negotiate a steep mountainside above the timberline.

29 A bull elk sports a magnificent spread of antlers as it grazes in a high valley.

30/31 Dazzling blue Peyto Lake, as seen from above Bow Summit. Glacial melt gives the alpine lakes of the Rockies their distinctive turquoise blue colour.

32 A proud climber poses atop Mount Lefroy, with a legion of Rocky Mountain peaks as a backdrop.

33 A crampon-clad mountaineer makes his way along the icy ridge of Mount Victoria.

34/35 The cerulean waters of Bow Lake, north of Lake Louise.

36 Mount Rundle and Vermilion Lakes, near Banff townsite.

37 top A splendid panoramic view of Mount Hector, Hector Lake, and Margaret Lake (foreground).

37 bottom Late afternoon sunshine reflects on the Bow River.

38 The Chateau Lake Louise has lured visitors for over a century with its superb lakeside situation.

39 Lake Minnewanka, with Mount Inglismaldie towering above, is a centre for power boaters and fishermen.

40 The Icefields Parkway winds for 230 km (143 mi) around lakes and mountains and climbs through high passes between Lake Louise and Jasper townsite, in Jasper National Park.

41 The jagged rock of Mount Wilson, wreathed in clouds.

42/43 Moraine Lake, in the Valley of Ten Peaks, is a classic Rockies scene.

JASPER

Jasper is Canada's largest national park, extending for 10,800 sq km (4200 sq mi) northwest of Banff National Park. Ninety-two percent of its area is high country—rugged mountains, alpine meadows, and vast glaciers, the largest of which is the Columbia Icefield, at 325 sq km (125 sq mi). The remoteness of much of the park makes it an ideal refuge for wildlife. Black bear, elk, bighorn sheep, and mountain goats are relatively plentiful in the high elevations. Jasper townsite, in the Athabasca Valley, provides tourist amenities while retaining its small-town charm.

The park is named for Jasper Hawes, a trapper for the North West Company who established a trading post on Brulé Lake on the Athabasca River in 1812. 'Jasper House' became an important supply station for trappers and traders traversing the Rockies via the Athabasca Pass, discovered two years earlier by David Thompson. The pass was later used by gold-rushers on their way to the Cariboo Valley. The upper Athabasca basin became Jasper National Park in 1907.

On the south end of the park, extending into Banff and British Columbia, is the Columbia Icefield, so huge that it feeds six large glaciers, including Athabasca, Dome, and Stutfield, which can be seen from the Icefields Parkway. Tourists who want a close-up view of the icefields can take a Snowcoach ride or an ice-walk tour.

Magnificent scenery greets the traveller going north on the parkway through the Athabasca Valley. Roads branch off and lead to Sunwapta Falls, Mount Edith Cavell and Angel Glacier, Maligne Lake, Celestine Lake, and Miette Hot Springs. The thundering Athabasca Falls lies south of Jasper townsite, just off the highway. North of town, Patricia and Pyramid lakes offer fishing and boating. Cross-country skiers and hikers head for the broad Tonquin Valley, overlooked by the imposing peaks of The Ramparts and studded with the sparkling Amethyst Lakes. The top of Whistlers Mountain (named for the whistling marmots who live there) yields a panoramic view of Jasper, with towering Mount Robson to the west and the bulk of the Columbia Icefield to the south.

Over 1000 km (600 mi) of hiking trails criss-cross the park. Trail riding, bicycling, canoeing, and white water rafting are other popular summer pursuits. In winter Marmot Basin attracts skiers with 33 challenging runs, and for those with the skill, courage, and money, heli-skiing is an exciting way to experience the peace of Jasper's pristine wilderness.

45 The great plunge of Athabasca Falls into a deep gorge, 32 km (20 mi) south of Jasper townsite.

46/47 Maligne Lake is the largest glacier-fed lake in the Canadian Rockies, at 21 km (13 mi) long. Boat trips journey to the mystical Spirit Island, which seems to hover in the intense blue waters of the lake.

48/49 The broad, high Tonquin Valley, a popular destination for hikers and, in winter, cross-country skiers.

50 Trail riders are dwarfed by the imposing peaks of The Ramparts as they skirt the Amethyst Lakes on their way through the Tonquin Valley.

51 Backcountry skiing on Jonas Pass, in the southern reaches of the park.

52/53 Mount Edith Cavell casts its snowy reflection into Cavell Lake.

54/55 Wildflowers such as yellow violets (left), moss campion (top), and phlox (below) abound in Jasper's wilderness in the summer months.

56/57 Surrounded by some of the highest peaks in the Canadian Rockies, the gigantic Columbia Icefield rises high above the scenic Icefields Parkway. The Athabasca Glacier tumbles down behind the Columbia Icefield Chalet.

58 Alpenglow lights up Mounts Columbia and King Edward in the Columbia Icefield area.

59 A halo encircles the winter sun as it rises over
a chain of high peaks in Jasper's remote backcountry.

60 A top-of-the-world view from the summit or Whistlers Mountain.

61 The still waters of Maligne Lake are painted in pastel hues at sundown.

62/63 Hikers on Parker's Ridge photograph the massive flow of the Saskatchewan Glacier, an arm of the Columbia Icefield.

64 The Columbian ground squirrel is native to the
region and can be found in meadow areas at all
altitudes throughout the Canadian Rockies.

65 Mule deer are plentiful in Jasper. This female
is seen with her two fawns in the spring.

66 *Mount Edith Cavell and Cavell Lake, cloaked in winter white.*

67 *Icicles decorate Athabasca Falls in cold blue and white in winter.*

WATERTON LAKES, YOHO, AND KOOTENAY

The colourful mountains of Waterton Lakes National Park, in the southwest corner of Alberta on the Montana border, spring up sharply from the rolling plains to the east, the result of ancient glacial activity which carved out deep valleys and left jagged mountain peaks. The sedimentary rock here is some of the oldest in the Canadian Rockies, recording a billion years of geological history. Upper Waterton Lake is the deepest in the Canadian Rockies at 148 m (485 ft) and contains unique marine life such as pygmy whitefish and opossum shrimp. Although measuring only 518 sq km (200 sq mi), the park's varied habitats support rich populations of flora and fauna.

Established in 1895, Waterton Lakes was joined to Glacier National Park in Montana in 1932 to create Waterton-Glacier International Peace Park, representing peace and good will along the longest undefended border in the world. Cameron Lake and Red Rock Canyon are picturesque destinations in Waterton Lakes, and of the many waterfalls that grace the park, the cascading Cameron Falls is one of the most accessible. The stately Prince of Wales Hotel occupies a stunning position on a bluff overlooking the lake, surrounded by majestic mountains.

On the west slope of the Rockies, in British Columbia, is Yoho National Park, appropriately named for the Cree word for 'wonderful!' East of Banff and north of Kootenay, it comprises the upper valley of the Kicking Horse River. In only 1300 sq km (500 sq mi), the park contains some of the finest scenery in all of the Rockies, including 28 peaks over 3000 m (9800 ft), one of Canada's highest waterfalls, the 380-m (1247-ft) Takakkaw Falls, and more than 25 alpine lakes, filled with glacial melt, which shine an unforgettable turquoise blue in the sharp mountain sunshine. The park's highest peak, Mount Goodsir, soars to 3562 m (11,686 ft).

Just across the Continental Divide from Banff, Yoho boasts the same quality of alpine scenery with a fraction of the crowds. Road access to many of the natural attractions is limited; Lake O'Hara, just over the Divide from Lake Louise, is easily equal in splendour to its popular sister but is eight miles away from the nearest car park. Four hundred kilometres (250 mi) of trails thread through a network of cirque basins which hold gemlike lakes beneath steep mountains of rock, blue ice, and snow. Take the time to rest beside one of these lakes, gaze at the reflections of the mighty mountains on the smooth blue surface, and enjoy the tranquillity of nature at its very best.

Kootenay, also on the west slope of the Rockies in British Columbia, is bounded by Yoho on the north, Banff on the east and Mount Assiniboine Provincial Park on the southeast. Its 1406 sq km (543 sq mi) are composed of the lush green valleys of the Vermilion and Kootenay rivers and the surrounding high country. Marble Canyon, Redwall Fault, Kaufman Lake (across the Divide from Moraine Lake in Banff), and Floe Lake (named for the icebergs which break from the glacier on its western shore) are notable natural features. Large mammals can be seen at the animal lick near the Simpson River. The mineral baths at Radium Hot Springs, near the park's west entrance, lure weary tourists with their soothing waters.

69 Climbers scale the snowdrifts of Abbotts Pass
in Yoho National Park.

72/73 Yellow wildflowers stand in bright contrast
to the deep blue of Lake McArthur in Yoho.

70/71 Larches cling to a peninsula in beautiful
Floe Lake in Kootenay National Park.

74 top *This view over Carthew Lakes shows the colourful rock of which the mountains in Waterton Lakes National Park are made.*

74 bottom *The Prince of Wales Hotel, built in 1926, is situated on a bluff overlooking the Waterton Lakes.*

75 *Although bison no longer roam freely in the Canadian Rockies, a small herd can be seen at the Buffalo Paddocks in Waterton Lakes National Park.*

76/77 *The breathtaking vista of Waterton Lakes, with the Prince of Wales Hotel in the centre.*

78/79 *Without the trees the hard gray rock of the Opabin Plateau in Yoho would look like a moonscape.*

80 Takakkaw Falls in Yoho freefalls for 380 metres (1247 feet), making it one of the highest in Canada.

81 The Elizabeth Parker Mountain Hut huddles beneath majestic Cathedral Mountain in Yoho.

82/83 Floe Lake in Kootenay catches the reflection of alpine larches and evergreens in its cold waters.

84 A skier enjoys a birds-eye view of the peaks above Lake O'Hara in Yoho.

85 Sunset bathes Cathedral Mountain in Yoho in a purple glow.

86/87 Evidence of ancient glacial activity is everywhere at Lake Oesa in Yoho. The cirque basin filled with glacial melt, the loose dirt on the shore, and the carved and sculpted mountains above it are typical of alpine lakes in the park and throughout the Canadian Rockies.

88/89 Beautiful Lake O'Hara in Yoho lies beneath the same two mountains—Victoria and Lefroy—which tower over Lake Louise in Banff, on the other side of the Continental Divide.

PROVINCIAL PARKS IN THE ROCKIES

Few tourists venture into the provincial parks in the Rockies since most are either out of the way or have limited or no road access. Set aside by the provincial governments as areas of outstanding scenic beauty, they present pockets of untouched alpine wilderness which are well worth the effort required to reach them.

Mount Robson Provincial Park in British Columbia, adjacent to Jasper in Alberta, contains the headwaters of the Fraser River and the highest peak in the Canadian Rockies, the 3954-m (12,972-ft) Mount Robson. Mountaineers find the climb to the summit a challenge, but hikers can glimpse the mountain from below through its ever-present veil of clouds as they walk the 22 km (14 mi) along the Robson River, past Kinney Lake and the Valley of a Thousand Falls to Berg Lake. Berg Glacier, one of the few advancing glaciers in the Rockies, regularly heaves icebergs into the lake. The sheer north face of Robson rises 2400 m (7800 ft) from the shores of the lake, a dramatic sight and a great reward. The rest of the 2178 sq km (838 sq mi) of the park supports sizeable populations of wildlife, alpine meadows bright with wildflowers in summer, and glaciated mountains typical of the Rockies.

The pride of Mount Assiniboine Provincial Park is its namesake, at 3618 m (11,870 ft) the seventh highest peak in the Canadian Rockies. Its distinctive pointed shape resembles Switzerland's Matterhorn, and it can easily be seen from high points in neighbouring Banff and Kootenay. However, getting a closer look entails at least a day's hike, as there is no road access to the park. Most visitors head for Lake Magog at the base of the mountain, where the Assiniboine Lodge is located. In the total park area of 386 sq km (149 sq mi), there is no ground less than 1524 m (5000 ft) high. Towering peaks, alpine meadows, and high valleys splashed with yellow alpine larch in autumn make Assiniboine a worthy destination for hardy hikers.

Lougheed is an exceptional provincial park in that it offers numerous recreational opportunities. Located south of Banff, in Alberta, the park is part of the 4000 sq-km (1540 sq-mi) Kananaskis Country, a region of mountains and foothills which is being used for resource development as well as recreation. Downhill skiers can enjoy their sport on Mount Allan and Fortress Mountain, and cross-country skiers can take advantage of a well-developed network of trails. Fishing, waterskiing, canoeing, and kayaking are popular on the region's many lakes and rivers. Golfers can choose from two 18-hole golf courses in a spectacular mountain setting. Accommodations range from five-star hotels to campgrounds.

Other provincial parks in the Rockies include Hamber, Top of the World, Elk Lakes, and Bow Valley.

91 The distinctive peak of Mount Assiniboine catches the early morning light.

92/93 *Mount Assiniboine and Sunburst Peak rise above Sunburst and Cerulean lakes, Mount Assiniboine Provincial Park, British Columbia.*

94 *Even in summer Mount Robson and its neighbouring peaks can be buried in deep snow.*

95 At 3954 m (12,972 ft), Mount Robson is the highest peak in the Canadian Rockies.

96 The high alpine meadows of Mount Robson Provincial Park in British Columbia are rich with wildflowers in the summer.

97 A burst of purple wildflowers in the lower elevations of the park.

98/99 Sunset lights up the mountain sky in pale gold and orange.

100/101 One of the 18-hole golf courses in Kananaskis Country, with fairways surrounded by towering peaks.

102 The view looking east from Burstall Pass, in the north part of Lougheed Provincial Park, Alberta.

103 White water rafting is one of the many sports enjoyed by outdoors enthusiasts in Kananaskis Country.

104/105 The Chester Lake area in the Kananaskis Valley, Lougheed Provincial Park.

106/107 Mount Assiniboine Provincial Park boasts some of the most spectacular scenery in the Rockies, but the park is accessible only by foot or helicopter.

THE COLUMBIAS

The Columbia Mountains form the most dramatic scenery of the British Columbia interior west of the Rocky Mountain Trench. Built of older, harder rock than the Rockies, this range is characterised by tightly packed, sharply pointed peaks divided by deep, narrow valleys. The Purcells, Selkirks, Monashees, and Cariboos, the subranges which make up the Columbias, draw mountaineers, skiers, and hikers with the promise of rugged, challenging terrain and a harsh, wild beauty unexcelled by the more popular range to the east.

Glacier National Park occupies 1334 sq km (513 sq mi) in the northern Selkirks. The 3390-m (11,123-ft) Mount Dawson is the park's highest point, and half of the park has an elevation of over 1800 m (6000 ft). One quarter of the area is permanently covered in ice and snow by over 100 glaciers. The infamous Rogers Pass (1288 m/4225 ft) once carried the Canadian Pacific Railway over the mountains, but frequent avalanches, which killed 200 people between 1885 and 1911, caused the railroad to go underground in 1916. Today, Highway 1 passes over Rogers Pass, but heavy snowfall often closes it during the long winter months.

Established in 1886 with the coming of the railroad, the park quickly drew courageous outdoorsmen eager to ascend the thrilling heights of the Sir Donald and Hermit ranges. In those days, visitors stayed in the railroad's luxurious Glacier House Hotel, near Rogers Pass. The hotel burned down in 1925, and the Glacier Park Lodge now provides accommodations for those keen to experience the natural grandeur of Glacier.

The chief attraction of Mount Revelstoke National Park, on the western slope of the Selkirks, is the 21-km (13-mi) gravel road which ascends 1938-m (6140-ft) Mount Revelstoke, yielding fabulous views across the Columbia Valley to the Monashees on the north, and the Selkirks on the east, with the city of Revelstoke spread out below. The road begins at an elevation of 600 m (1969 ft) in a dense rain forest and ends in alpine tundra near the treeline and just below the summit. Trails starting at the car park lead to blue alpine lakes and a closer view of the peaks of the Clachnacudainn Range and the massive Clachnacudainn Icefield.

The Purcells, which run from the US border to near Golden, British Columbia, offer largely untamed wilderness country of exceptional beauty to intrepid travellers. Climbers are attracted to the Bugaboos, a series of sheer granite spires thrust up through vast icefields. Howser Spire is the tallest, at 3399 m (11,150 ft), and the rest range between 2700 and 3300 m (9000 and 11,000 ft). The Purcell Wilderness Conservancy and the exquisite St Mary's Alpine Provincial Park also provide spectacular scenery, featuring clear blue lakes, knife-edge ridges, and deep glacial valleys.

West of the Selkirks rise the Monashees, where avid skiers take helicopters into the wilderness to enjoy the deep powder in winter. The Cariboos lie to the north, with 5200-sq-km (2000-sq-mi) Wells Gray Provincial Park framing a sizeable portion of the range. Mountains, glaciers, lakes, rivers, and waterfalls share space with extinct volcanoes and ancient lava flows. Ski touring from remote mountain chalets is popular in the Cariboos too, as it is throughout the remote, visually stunning Columbia Mountains.

109 At 3399 m (11,150 ft), Howser Spire is the tallest peak in the Bugaboos. The skier is mountaineer Pat Morrow, the second Canadian ever to reach the top of Mount Everest.

110/111 Golden alpine larch lines the shores of St Mary's Lake, in remote St Mary's Alpine Provincial Park in the Purcells.

112 Mountain goats are numerous in Glacier National Park in the northern Selkirks.

113 A black bear in a tree on the Mount Revelstoke Summit Road. Both the Rockies and the Columbias have large bear populations.

114 The sheer south face of Snowpatch Spire, in the Bugaboos in the northern Purcells, attracts rock climbers looking for a real challenge.

115 Orange Indian paintbrush is featured in the wild alpine meadows in the Boulder Camp area of Bugaboo Provincial Park.

116/117 Mount Sir Donald and other lofty peaks of the Sir Donald Range thrust their granite summits through a great mass of ice in dramatic Glacier National Park.

118/119 The breathtaking view from the summit of Mount Revelstoke, with the city of Revelstoke below in the Columbia Valley.

120/121 Intrepid climbers in Glacier are treated to views of toothlike peaks encased in ice.

122/123 Camping above timberline below the Quintet Peaks in the Purcell Mountains, near Kimberley.

124 Clouds hang below treacherous Rogers Pass in Glacier.

125 The thrill of ski touring in fresh powder in the Monashees.

126/127 Bare rock, glaciers, and snowfields make up the harsh yet beautiful landscape of the Bugaboos.